A Cute Mouse
and the
7 Deadly Cheeses

By Mavis E Robinson

ISBN-10:0648305902

ISBN-13:978-0648305903

ACKNOWLEDGMENTS

I WOULD LIKE TO THANK
THE WOODEND ART GROUP
FOR THEIR ADVICE AND SUPPORT,
ESPECIALLY THE TUESDAY SOCIAL GROUP,
FAMILY AND FRIENDS

THIS LITTLE BOOK OF MICE
IS DEDICATED TO THE
CHEESEMAKERS OF THE WORLD.

SLOTH

The Bogan

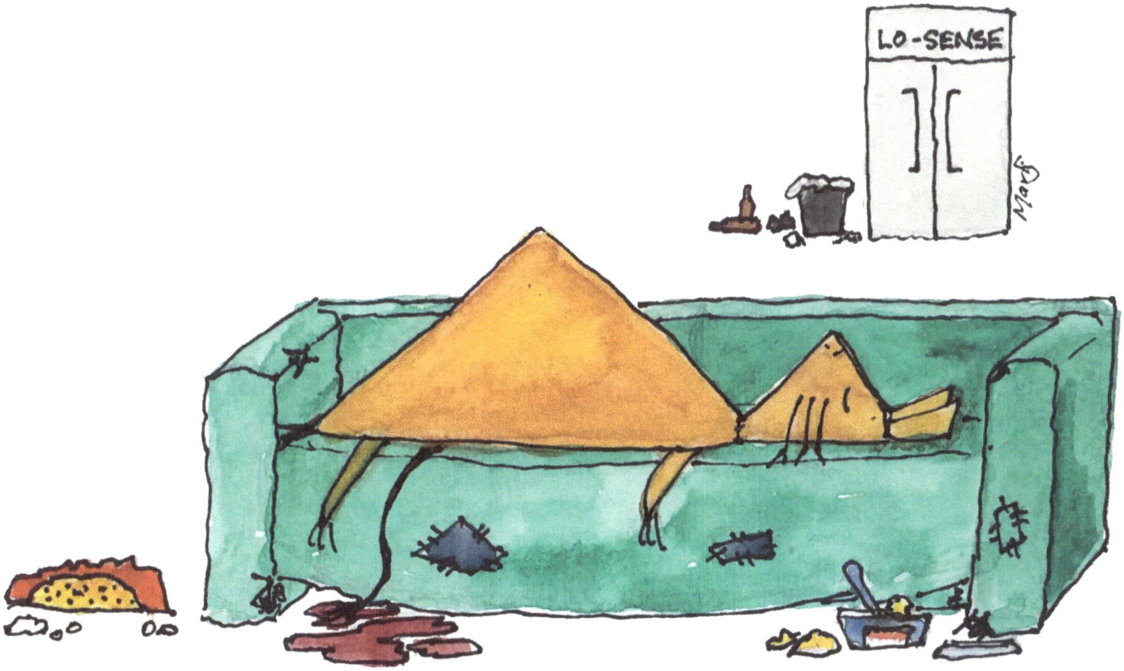
LO-SENSE

GLUTTONY

Processed Cheese

WRATH

Rat Rage

GREED

The Hoarder

THE CHEESE XCHANGE

LUST

Temptation

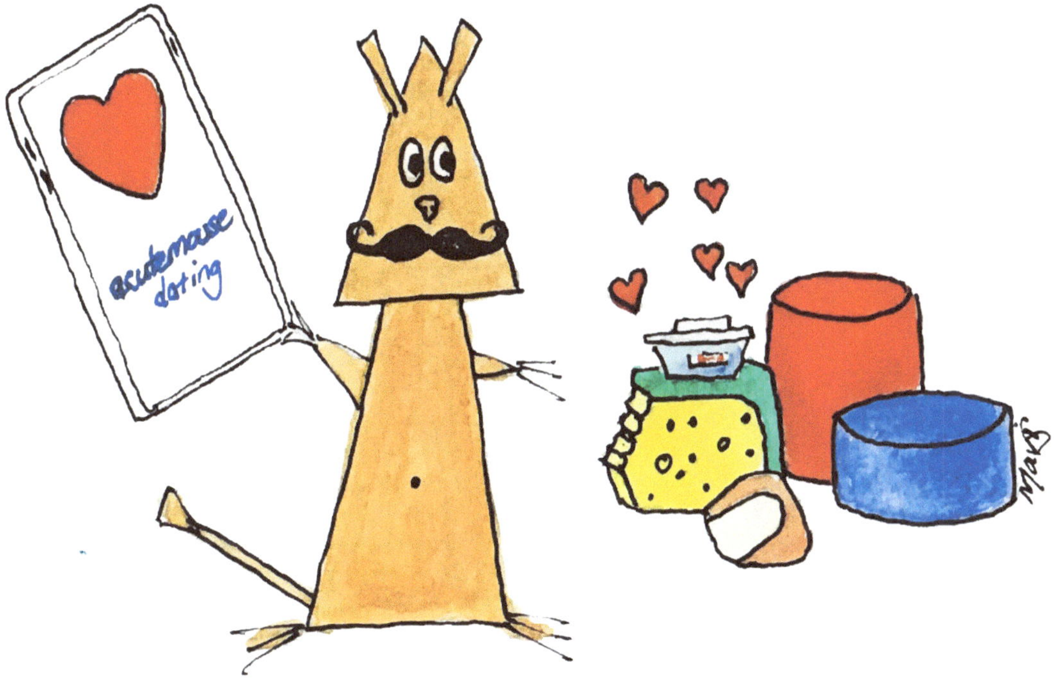
dating

VANITY

The Selfie

ENVY

The Jealous Guy

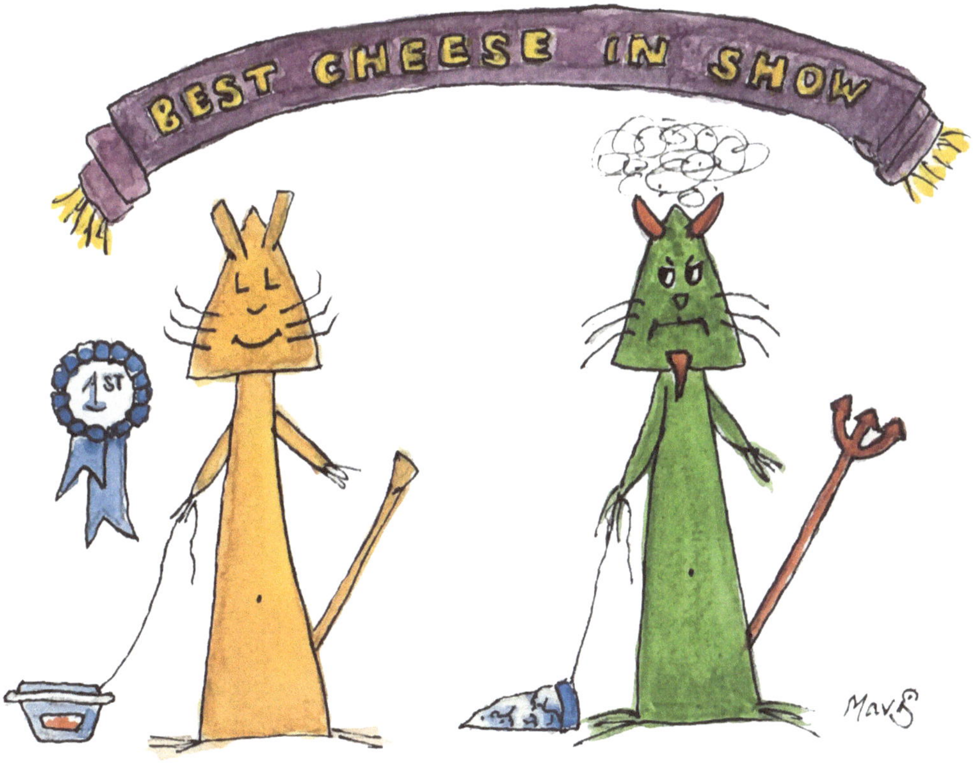
BEST CHEESE IN SHOW
1ST
Mav B

One virtue can make a difference...

CHARITY

The Holeless Shelter

CHEESE AND BLANKETS

It only takes one mouse to make the world a better place.

Which mouse will you be?

ABOUT THE AUTHOR

Mavis lives with her husband Colin and her cat called Lily
in a small town north of Melbourne, Victoria, Australia
where she enjoys creative pursuits.
This is her first book.

www.ingramcontent.com/pod-product-compliance
Lightning Source LLC
Chambersburg PA
CBHW060841270326
41933CB00002B/162

* 9 7 8 0 6 4 8 3 0 5 9 0 3 *